MY TALK – BOOK THIRTEEN

Just when I thought it was over, here comes another book.

Also note in book twelve I messed up in the book description in the other books by Michelle Jean section. Yes I am so lazy to change this so can you please change it for me. Yes you will have to find the mistake. It is noticeable if you are scrolling through the list of books that I've written.

Yes the imperfections are still there but I am hoping I get better and move closer to perfection where these books are totally error free. And James no, I cannot bring anyone into this as much as I want and need to. So no editors, no ghost writers, no one can help me. Not even the spirit world is allowed to. Complaints fall on deaf ears so I've learnt to live with my imperfections. But in truth perfections despite my massive limitations in the human and or physical and spiritual world. Listen, you'll know there are spelling mistakes and grammatical error. I've tried to catch them and fix them but I truly cannot catch all. Any ho, dreamt I was in this place working with Buju Banton (Mark Myrie). He was neatly dressed in a white shirt and I believe black pants. So I don't know if he's going to go to court again. But the section I was in and or working in was messy; thus a dream inna dream. I have to clean up the table in my house. Thus in the dream I was cleaning up and or organizing the table in my work area. I was rushing because I was running out of time.

There was a Chinese lady in the office and she was helping me to clean up. People I do not know where Shaggy came from, but in the dream I mistook him for Buju. I called him Buju in the dream and I corrected myself. He was in my bed and I went on the bed with him Shaggy. I told him how they set up Buju and how I tried to help by sending a message to someone and I was ignored. He Shaggy seemed uninterested as to the fact that they set up this man (Buju Banton). Thus no one truly cares. I told him Shaggy about the sword that they placed around and or on Buju so that he would die in prison. People I began to cry because it truly hurt me that someone would hurt another human being like this and no one in the upper echelon in the black community is doing anything to help this man. No one truly cares and this is sad and hurtful. There is something wrong about this whole Buju saga and no one is truly doing anything about it.

Listen, people talk and a note to the gay community, not everyone is gay, and not everyone is going to become gay. You cannot muzzle a man or woman including child if they truly do not like you.

We live in societies where people take it upon themselves to hate others by what they have been taught. Billions of us have been taught to hate by others including the religious leaders (clergy) of the world. They the clergy take it upon themselves to speak on the behalf of God when

Lovey did not commission any of them to speak on the behalf of Him. They the members of the clergy have and has overstepped their boundaries with their lies and deceit; thus they are all hell bound literally. Not one will be saved because they spread hate and tell lies on Life; Good God and Allelujah for whom I call Lovey because of truth and true love that is more than unconditional.

Blacks are hated globally but we do not put down that person, we let them be because the majority of us know the hell that person is going to face shortly.

*Humans hate what they cannot comprehend, so for you to sentence this man to death for his actions; not promoting gayness you are wrong. Yes I know the drug charge but someone took this too far. **This wrong must be corrected because the spiritual world is truly not letting it go. You all know the wrongs that you did, so truly free this man.***

There is something called freedom of speech and humans are free to express their feelings. So if you the gay community have any part in this, release this man because I am truly tired of seeing this injustice. Know that an innocent man was sent to prison and if justice is not done; this man released, then everyone associated with the case including the judge that sentenced him, ***AND THE ENTIRE GLOBAL GAY COMMUNITY will be condemned.*** I will not warn the people that did this again because when you are condemned, your entire family is condemned and it's not fair for you to take your entire family to hell with you.

There is a grave injustice that was done to this man and all of you who did this to this man can correct it.

You as the global gay community are being warned. Thus if you don't fix this mess and or if you are involved, then I WILL ENSURE ALL THAT IS WRITTEN IN THE BOOK WHAT A MESS BECOMES NULL AND VOID AS OF DECEMBER 2015. FIX IT AND NOW LEST YOU THE GAY COMMUNITY LOSE IT ALL GLOBALLY. This is not a threat or a promise. This is my word of truth, thus saith the Lord thy God meaning I will petition Lovey to condemn the lots of you and lock your asses more than infinitely and indefinitely out of his world and abode including kingdoms. Trust me I will petition him to make you the gay community like onto Sodom and Gomorrah thus destroying the lots of you. Fix it because He Lovey is giving you time to fix and or correct this mess.

Thus the obeah man or woman that crossed this man with the swords of death so that he dies in prison; there is absolutely no remission of sin for you because you crossed an innocent man for money. So you are truly condemned along with your family. So I commission you to uncross this man and plea for forgiveness in your own way so that your family and you may live.

Yes I said there is no remission for you but I am giving you a chance to rectify your wrong to this man. Lovey is giving all of you a chance before your condemnation takes shape and fold. Make right your wrong because it's not right for an innocent man to pay the price for your hate.

So as Shaggy and I lay in bed, I told him I know what he did. I told him that anyone that signs a pact with the devil, the devil owns them, owns their children and wife. He was surprised when I told him about the devil owning their wife. In the dream he was also telling me about Janet Jackson. Hence we know where it all began.

So it matters not if you are a lodge man or woman, the devil owns all of you. You and your entire family the devil owns and you cannot get out of this contract because you are truly hell bound.

It matters not if you are Free Mason

Illuminati

Scientologists

Satanist

Pagan

Shaman

Obeah Man or Woman

Voodoo Priest or Priestesses

Witches or Warlocks

Enchanters of the dead

It matters not if you feed the dead for favour. As long as you deal in the dead; evil, there is absolutely nothing you can do to save you and your family because you've commissioned them to hell with your actions. It matters not if you are a king or queen of your land. So long as you deal in the dead and with the dead your land and people belongs to death.

It matters not if you are a clergy member. So long and or as long as you go to church and worship the dead; a dead god and or man; you are condemned to hell, thus you belong to death. If you have family that you've baptized in death and have not repented of this sin, then your entire family belongs to death. They too are hell bound.

It's not wha or what. YOU SENTENCED YOUR ENTIRE FAMILY TO HELL WITH YOU. THUS NONE CAN SAVE YOU BECAUSE YOU TOOK THEIR RIGHT AND LIFE FROM THEM.

If a good family member truly loves you and depending on their good and evil record; meaning, if they have more good on their record; they can save you. It's not Lovey alone that can save you. Good people out there can save you. **_HOWEVER, IF YOU HAVE SIGNED A PACT WITH THE DEVIL; EVIL; LOVEY CANNOT SAVE YOU NOR CAN A GOOD PERSON WHETHER FAMILY OR OTHERWISE SAVE YOU._** *This is the law and it cannot be broken thus I tell you what belongs to death belongs to death both male and female. There is no Jesus to call on because I explained to you in book twelve of the MY TALK series who Jesus represented. All of humanity got it wrong when it came to Jesus thus hell is full of all NATIONALITIES.*

Man did the lie stick.

So for all of you people who join lodges and secret societies, know this as of September 08, 2015 there is ABSOLUTELY NO REMISSION OF SIN FOR YOU AND YOUR FAMILY. ALL YOUR NAMES ARE WRITTEN IN DEATH'S BOOK. THERE IS NOTHING ANYONE CAN DO TO GET YOUR NAME, THE NAME OF YOUR CHILDREN AND SPOUSE AND OR SPOUSES OUT OF DEATH'S BOOK.

YOU ARE ALL SEALED WITH DEATH'S MARK THUS YOU ARE ALL HELL BOUND.

Lovey cannot save you because you truly belong to death. You are not a part of life because you gave all of you (your life) including the life of your loved ones to death; Satan. So as a part of Satan's world truly good luck because hell is truly waiting for you.

Yes she thanked me for outing everyone one by one and I think I gave her a colour in one of these books. I think I said she was white but originally she had no hue. So forgive me for giving her a colour status.

It's beyond me why anyone would say they love their family and sentence them to hell. But then again, love is hate in my world. There is no truth in love thus man; humanity knows not about true love.

I will reiterate this again. ***IT'S THE ONES THAT SAY THEY LOVE YOU THAT SCREW UP YOUR LIFE AND TAKE YOUR GOOD AND TRUE LIFE AWAY FROM YOU.***

Thus it's the ones that say they love you that send you straight to hell to burn brutally and afterwards die.

Every man woman and child has a saving grace, but the ones that say they love us, take this saving grace from us. Why?

If you say you love me; then love me true.

Do not hate me and say you love me.

Do not smile with me and pretend to like me.

Do not come near me then. If you cannot truly love me then don't come around me.

If you cannot truly love me, don't stay with me. Keep your lies and fake self and attitude to yourself.

TRUE FRIENDS DO NOT BREAK YOU DOWN. TRUE FRIENDS BUILD WITH EACH OTHER THUS TRUE LOVE ALL AROUND.

But yet in this world, humans on a whole cannot see this

When one try to rise you break them down.

I do not like what you say thus I am going to show you who has more power and strength.

Who has authority and control over whom?

Did God and or Lovey give you authority and control over me?

No he did not. But yet you want to control me and all around me.

Don't try to control me because you have no authority over you. **_No human being on the face of this planet has control over their own spirit; self. The spirit is a part of a collective that can and is controlled by a greater and higher force._** No you are not a puppet, hence you have free will. The spirit has a source; thus that source is good or evil depending on the choice that you make at and yes before birth. **_No,_** it's not you that make that choice, your family; mother and father made that choice for you before birth and at birth. And yes this has a lot to do with cleanliness, thus many are called but the chosen are few.

Can we put down our dirty ways and become clean?

Yes for many, but for many others they cannot become clean because they were born under the order of death literally. Thus evil cannot become clean because he or she is true evil.

So Lovey and her; your message has and have been delivered.

The end is here for all wicked and evil systems globally. Now tell me, who's going to become extinct?

Die for wants and needs; food and water.

If I don't like you, it's my right not to like you. No, I cannot say I don't like you because someone tell me not to like you. It's wrong for me to do this, but it's also wrong to strangle a person and take away their freedom.

Thus shortly humanity is truly going to suffer for the wrongs they have done.

I cannot tell you which airport this happened in but I dreamt there was a mid air collision with two planes. All I know is; no, not all I know. In the dream the pilot of one of the planes was black with long dreadlocks. He looked like someone I know in real life. He the black pilot was at fault in the dream. He flew right into the next plane. I cannot tell you if all white people was onboard the next plane but white people were furious. Said, how stupid (dumb) could he be. The plane was right there. How could he not see?

So somewhere in my view, Black Death is going to claim the lives of people in mid air. And my true family and people it does not necessary mean it's a black pilot. Black Death does have dreadlocks. You know what. I am going to leave it because it was a black man with dreadlocks flying the plane. And no people, he the black pilot did not die in the dream. He walked out of the plane unhurt. He was okay. Please figure it out for me because like I've told you time and time again in so many of my other books. Death will mask death when death does not want to let go of its spoil. Meaning death wants those lives; have to take them because they belong to him or her. So they won't show you where death is going to come from.

And no you cannot say well I am not going to fly. Death patiently waits sometimes. If it takes 30 years for you to take flight death will wait. Hey death has time.

Don't go there because death hath time and death is in time also.

But Satan lost when it comes to God and or Lovey.

Yes, but when it came to man; humanity, Satan won.

And no, Satan is not death even though we interchange the two. See Satan has no say in hell. He may have the say over you on earth because you gave him authority to due to your sins and acceptance of him, but in hell Satan has no say.

And no Satan is not more powerful than death because it is death that takes his life; the life of Satan.

Oh man I have to write another JUST ONE OF THOSE DAYS book. Got to vent in a different way.

Yes it's September 08 and I so don't know what else to write. As the day progresses we will see. So until later, truly take care. AND IF YOU KNOW SOMEONE THAT KNOWS BUJU BANTON AND HIS FAMILY, PLEASE SEE THAT THAT HEAR ABOUT THIS BOOK AND OR GIVE THEM THE MESSAGE. Like I said, my spirit is not letting this case rest. I truly need true and proper closure for this man. So if you can truly help, please truly help because something is truly not right. Come on now help the man. I don't know him and for me to being seeing Him (Buju) again tells me something. Hence I've delivered your message yet again Lovey. So please open the right and true doors for this man to be free. Yes there is a critical change coming and if you can help do the right thing. Please do so.

Michelle Jean

Man yesterday I wrote about the planes crashing in mid air and I saw on MSN this morning (September 09) that a plane caught fire in mid air.

Wow.

I am so going to leave things at this.

Dreamt I had a new born baby. The baby had a light blue cap on. In the dream it was like I went home; was in Jamaica and I wanted to go to a party that was held at my grandmother's house. In the dream it was my son's family that was keeping the party. Suffice to say, I went parting and came home. I was going through my last draw; dresser draw that had all baby stuff in it. I was throwing things out and that's when I saw the baby lying face down in urine and soggy diaper. The baby looked blue in the face as if it was dying and or close to death. When I saw the baby that was when I remembered that I had a baby. People and family, in the dream I partied hard; had lots of fun. Stripping the baby naked, the baby had rash marks on its stomach because it was wet and lying there in urine. Hurrying now I took my left breast out and started to feed the baby, but the baby kept spitting my breast out and you could see the thick rich creamy milk in its mouth. He did not want the left breast so I gave the baby the right breast and the baby drank but not much. The baby did not want this breast either, but instead played with my right beast in its mouth. After that, I took the baby to the bathroom and washed him off in his white blanket. I believe my son came into the bathroom and asked me a question. I believe the question was, "what are you doing?" then he left. Yes I know what this dream means but I am so going to leave things alone. What do not concern you leave it alone and I am so leaving things alone.

I know lies and until I get the full truth, then this dream truly do not concern me. Yes the emotions are all over the place and I am so going to keep this as is because I am one stubborn person. On certain things I will not rock nor will I move. The words of man, I will not let faze me or move me. There is something not right in my personal life. Well not my personal life, but my son's personal life and until I hear the truth from both sides, I will leave them alone because trouble nuh set like rain.

Trouble a come; serious trouble, and a child is involved; going to get hurt. Yes I will warn my son of the dangers because like I said, mi pickney dem nuh listen to good counsel. Like I've said in many of my other books, dem stubban and haadeease. They have the source and refuse the source. So all I can do is walk away from them real soon so that they can fall on their own swords. As a parent; single mom, I can only do so much. You try to raise yu pickney dem right and they are the ones to come and bring you shame and disgrace.

Instead of helping dem a add more fuel to the fire. Suh dem want bun, fiya a goh bun dem. Soon I will be outta here and wey dem a guh du?

Ole people sey, wanti wanti caane get eee an getti getti nuh want it. An when trouble cum yu a si dem blame everybody under the sun. Just like many black in society blame white people for what happened to us. So as a parent, if you've done all you can, you have to learn to walk away from your ungrateful and hard ears children. They do not want your good counsel, give your good counsel to those that truly want and need it. This is what I am going to do; need to do and Lovey knows this. This is also what Lovey did to us as a race of people. He's tried and we are the ones that are not listening; so he's left us alone to our own choosing.

Yes this is disheartening on our part and on his part but I totally get it. He can't do everything for us. It would be nice but he cannot. Yes I told my son to pray and he said, "he's not praying because he does not believe in God. God does not help him and he can't believe in a God that is not there." I told him I will not try to convince him otherwise. His belief is his belief and I have to respect his beliefs.

As humans we are expecting Lovey to fix our wrongs for us and he cannot do that because our wrongs are not his wrongs. It is only when we do something that is inappropriate and or wrong that we are running to him to fix our issues. Many of us got warnings and many of us did not listen. Yes I know some of us cannot comprehend these warnings but Lovey did try. We just could not hear him properly thus we comprehended him and or what he was trying to tell us wrong. Not one of us realizes self. We go on doing wrongs like they are the in thing, and when things blow up in our faces we go running and a crying to Lovey. We say he's not fair because he allowed evil to befall us. We've forgotten that the wages of sin is death and when we go against Lovey and his truths bad things do happen to us. When we disobey the demons of hell step in and they can do whatever they want to do with you; us. Yes I know not all of us do wrong thus the evils that some people do unto others. Man to man is unjust thus demons inflict severe pain on us.

My son did wrong and I told him this. I told him God cannot forgive him of his sins because he did not sin against God.

I told him I forgave them (all my children) of all the wrongs they've done to me and maybe Lovey is waiting on him to say sorry. I told him not everyone can forgive you of your wrongs to them and that is okay.

**Family and People, God and or Lovey cannot sin you or hold not forgiving a person against you because he Lovey truly do not forgive all.** It is your right to forgive or not to forgive. _And no, no one can forgive a person on your behalf._ **_NO MAN WOMAN OR CHILD CAN FORGIVE YOUR SINS BECAUSE NO ONE ON THE FACE OF THIS PLANET HAS THAT AUTHORITY TO DO SO. NOT EVEN LOVEY HIMSELF._**

Lovey cannot take your sins from your sin record and or plate but yet each and every day you have some members *of the clergy putting themselves above God and or Lovey and saying your sins are forgiven.*

So yes my son did wrong and I will not petition Lovey for him because that would be wrong on my part. His wrongs are his wrongs and it would wrong of me to go to Lovey and say, forgive him. Yes I can, hence my wording is incorrect.

I CANNOT IN GOOD FAITH PETITION LOVEY AND SAY MAKE MY SON'S WILLFUL WRONGS RIGHT. I CANNOT DO THAT NOR WILL I EVER DO THAT. MY SON DID MAKE A CHOICE AND HE MUST LIVE BY THIS CHOICE FOR THE REST OF HIS LIFE. He was duly warned and he said, "he's not listening to me because she was his choice."

Yes the pressure is there and I am caught up in this because he lives with me, but I truly cannot take the pressure because it's affecting my health literally. I truly cannot take the chest pains and I've told him this.

I've told him there is something not right in all of this; thus I am seeing her family on a regular now in my dream world and I truly do not want to. I truly don't need to because the lifeline and cord is cut by me. Sad yes, but don't come to me with lies and think I am going to find favour in you and with you. I know you are not clean so why should I let you into my world that I am trying to make clean. Thus the dirty will always seek occupancy amongst clean. Therefore, clean will always become dirty seeka dirty and unclean people.

Clean can no longer give rise and or way to unclean. Like I've said in some of my other books, evil cannot change and will never change. There is no good in evil and we all know this, but yet humanity has compassion for the wicked and evil of this world. Yes I know my dream is a dream inna dream and my son have to clean up his act because unclean spirits do walk with him and it's a shame. No, I did not tell you the dream thus let sleeping dogs lay as we humans would say.

In life we have to own up to our wrongs and we cannot blame Lovey for them because like I said, Lovey did not commit our sins for us. We made them; committed them, so we have to clean up our self. We are the ones to dirty life and we are the ones that must clean life.

Yes it's unfortunate that he said what he said, but this is his belief like I've said. Yes I've talked to Lovey and **_he Lovey have to live with the consequences of hearing both young and old say they don't believe in him._** He Lovey made this love hate and or good and evil escapade escalate. He Lovey did not build impenetrable frameworks and foundations with his good and true people. So he Lovey has to face his own turmoil and deal with it. I cannot deal with it for him because it was him that made this mess. He sacrificed good to evil for a time and that was wrong of him. Yes this is his pain and he must live with this pain of knowing that some of his creation turned from him. No child and or no one and or anyone should have to say they don't believe in him Lovey; God due to hurt and pain. Belief changes I know. I know knowledge and I know him. Knowledge cannot change hence we know this I know.

Yes there were and still are consequences to his actions and he has to live with them like I said.

No father or mother should have to hear, "I don't believe in you, you are not real because you cannot help them." I've always said every child needs a mother and father, but he Lovey chose to walk away from his own due to sin; cleanliness. Yes things did change over the course of time; history, but it did not mean he should have abandoned us in this way. Yes he's tried to help, but truly how much help? No, I will not go there because I know how much help he tried to give thus these books for real. He did send others; we as humans were the ones to reject them because they did not fit our pathetic and egotistical profile of greed and immorality.

As parents if we cannot teach right, how are your children going to become right; know right from wrong?

If all we are getting is false teaching, will we not grow up to believe in these false teachings?

Will we not carry on the traditions of falsehood?

You as a father and mother cannot say you love your children so and leave them in undesirable situations. Therefore, I will always say love is hate because it's the ones that say they love you that truly hurt you royally; badly.

It's the ones that say they love you that keep you shackled and chained; dying for hunger, want and need.

It's the ones that say they love you that use and abuse you; leave you in a pool of blood for dead.

Yes there are psychological issues that impact our spirit and Lovey knows this, but yet find it hard to address these issues openly. So in all that he created we as humans can say he created ugly; imperfect.

In many ways and to me only; he cannot say well you did wrong and you should know better. This is wrong on his part because he allowed sin into our lives in the first place. Further, if we as humans do not have the full and true truth we will continue to do wrong.

We will continue down our hateful, spiteful and sinful pathway.

So yes I will not blame all on sin because in my book and view; Lovey is to blame also. Yes he's walked away from humanity and to me this is petty on his part. He wants us to be clean and live clean and when we go to him for help we are ignored. So what does he expect? Will we not turn to evil when he ignores us?

Will we not accept the offerings of evil when he ignores us?

Will we not seek affection and truth from someone else? Is this not what many in society have and has done?

So how can you blame us for sin WHEN TRUTH WAS NEVER FULLY THERE, NOR WAS THE FULL TRUTH GIVEN?

No child deserves pain. No one deserves pain because pain leaves us broken, wanting and needing and Lovey knows this. Thus he too must begin to amend for his wrongs; dirty ways. He cannot out us out without outing self. Come on now.

He does not like pain, so why should we as humans like pain?

He does not like to be hurt, so why should we like hurt?

Why should we be used and abused brutally because of his unjust ways?

Yes we are punished for our wrongs, but why should sin be involved in our lives if we have and has chosen Him Lovey?

Should he not close the doors and windows to sin?

Yes I have many questions as always; thus Lovey do think and read the words in these books in his and her own way.

WE CAN ALL BLAME, BUT IN TRUTH, WE AS HUMANS ARE TO BLAME FOR OUR OWN SINS. DESPITE THE LIES, THE TRUTH IS OUT THERE, WE WERE THE LAZY ONES TO NOT SEEK THE TRUTH FOR OUR OWN SELF.

Thus I will tell the black race, when you accept another nation's culture, history, race and name, you've given up yours. Thus your name is in their book and not the Black Book; Book of Life. This is why many nations can say BLACK PEOPLE WERE NOT IN EGYPT, EUROPE, RUSSIA, ICELAND, CHINA, MONGOLIA AND MORE. It matters not the monuments that are still standing that depicts us, we were never there. How name and history has and have become theirs because we as black people gave up our rights to them time and time again literally.

Now tell me, what ancestral black names do we have in this day and time?

Do not come to me with Mohammed or Mustafa or Zaid, or Rashida, or Zaykwuan, or Dayquan or Fatima to name a few. These are not black name and or of the origin of Black. They are Babylonian names, hence Blacks were colonized by Babylon long before Adam and Eve. As blacks we say we know our history, roots and culture. But I say unto you, we know not our roots and culture; true story and or history due to colonization and accepting Babylonian own.

So to you that are saying you are trying to justify your son's actions. I say unto you, I will not justify my child. He did wrong and when you do wrongs you have to pay the consequences of them just like Lovey is doing. We hurt him because he too did wrong in my view.

Yes I strayed off topic and went ahead of myself. Thus I am toggling dates because it's September 10, and many of this was written yesterday.

Onwards I go.

Everyone thinks we are all from Africa when not all black people come from Africa.

Like I said, when you give up your name; family name and accept another man's name and culture, you've lost yours. You as a man and or person have no more lineage and or future and or culture because his lineage becomes your lineage. This is what black people did long before Adam and Eve. Our ancestors gave up their language, name and identity and accepted Babylonian history and culture and this is why when you ask certain Egyptians about blacks in Egypt, they are quick to tell you black people never existed in Egypt. It's like the question you ask them becomes a curse word and or a curse to them.

Thus the fighting will never stop and the different races will forever tell you that the black race is the inferior race.

They tell us we do not belong. And in fact we do not belong because we were the ones to give up our true and natural own to accept their name, customs, pagan and nasty ways.

Look at Africa today. They know not who they are thus the different crap that is happening in Africa. Ask an African about their true language and identity, they cannot tell you because Babylon customs and trends are engrained in all that they do and they do not realize it. And if you try and tell them this, they will not listen to you.

Creole French, Arabic which comes from Urdu which is another dialect of Sanscript was never our original language, nor was Spanish or Portuguese. Nor was English. The original language of the black man was none of these languages. Actually, we've lost our original language and only a selected few can write this language.

We were the original creators and builders of this earth and universe but when you tell people this, they frown on you. They can only quote the diluted crap that was given to them that said, we were slaves and I am truly tired of this crap. Tired of the lies being told on the black race.

God and or Lovey did not make slaves. Humans turned other humans into slaves.

Every race on the face of this planet has and have stolen from the black man; race.

Down to the Jesus that they serve they stole because their so called holy book described Jesus in revelations as being black with nappy as pappy hair.

Everything we create they steal. Thus the black man cannot have anything because our identity has been taken from us. We cannot prosper because of some of these identity thieves.

You don't like us so stop stealing our identity then.

Stop taking the credit for what we design and create.

Do for you and stop stealing from us come on now.

And for you lying kiss mi ass Europeans that keep saying blacks were never in Europe. Truly go bleep yourselves. Everywhere on the face of this planet housed black people. BLACKS LIVED IN EUROPE LONG BEFORE YOU CAME INTO EXISTANCE. SO DON'T TAKE WHAT TRULY BELONG TO US AND TRY TO USE IT AGAINST US.

Life begets life and we've been creating life long before the first black man was put on this earth.

Life, true life is not hue. So keep your superiority bullshit BECAUSE WHITES CREATED NOTHING ON THIS PLANET. YOUR RACE IS SEPARATED FROM US. WE AS BLACKS DID NOT SEPARATE YOU, IT WAS YOUR CHOICE TO SEPARATE YOURSELF FROM US THUS YOU WERE NEVER IN THE BEGINNING WITH US.

AND IF YOU GO BACK TO THE FOUNDATION OF LIFE WHICH IS BLACK; BLUE WAS GIVEN BIRTH TO THEN WHITE FOLLOWED SUIT.

BLACK WAS FIRST FROM A COLOUR PERSPECTIVE AND YOU CANNOT CHANGE THIS.

IT WAS OUT OF THE BLACKNESS, DARKNESS OF LIFE THAT BLUE CAME AND THEN YOU CAME. SO TO SAY WHITES ARE SUPERIOR; KISS IT BECAUSE IT WAS OUT OF THE BLACK RACE YOU CAME. WE PUSHED YOUR RACIST ASSES OUT OF OUR VIJAY JAY AND THAT NONE OF YOU CAN CHANGE.

Thus not one of you are pure blood. Why don't the lots of you go back and check the true lineage of man if you can. The Chinese have more say than you because like I've said in my other books; at the base of the mountain of Lovey were Blacks and Chinese. You came in at the second stage in life.

So to all you racist bastards that are calling black people mutts (dogs) and monkeys are calling self mutts (dogs) and monkeys because it was a mutt (dog), and monkey the lots of you came from.

So yes the black race produced, gave birth to mutts and monkeys, YOU. And that you can truly call racist.

You want to separate yourself from the black race, go right ahead because at the end of the day whether you like it or not, it was a BLACK GOD that gave the lots of you life.

You can hate the black race all you want; I truly do not care because at the end of the day, whether you and the black race like it or not. YOU ARE IDENTICAL; TWINS; A TRUE FAMILY. Thus twincredibles that is floating around on the internet. YOU NEED US, WE DON'T NEED YOU PERIOD.

So it's family fighting against family.

Also know this; our skin tone represents death; physical and spiritual death. So truly take your racism and stick it because if you think your skin tone makes you a person you are truly pathetic fi real.

Yes I am dreaming about her church again. Cannot tell you the dream because this dream is a blur.

Dreamt about my brother. Dreamt he was at my home so I know he's not coming home anytime soon.

In the dream he cooked rice, white rice with ackee and salfish with calaloo and it was delicious. My daughter got some and I got some. I sat down to eat and did eat some of the food. He asked me how the food tasted and I told him delicious. When I told him that, I almost dropped my plate but caught it.

I don't know, but they say green; well green fruits is disappointment, so I guess I was eating disappointment even though it was not a fruit I was eating but calaloo.

I was saying I wanted to write another JUST ONE OF THOSE DAYS books because I saw something that I wanted to go ballistic on and cannot do it in this book due to language content. But I am so going to do it in this book anyway.

I was surfing the net yet again. Family and people you know I surf the net for everything that is of interest to me.

Mr. Vegas I find myself watching your posts on the internet. You had uploaded a file for which you deleted you were saying. Sorry you had to do it. _But let me correct you on something. Jamaica on a whole and not just in the_ _music industry, but the entire island ON A WHOLE HAS AND HAVE BEEN PLAGUED WITH PEDOPHILES._

You have grown ass men raping little girls. Some families get hush money an kip quiet and some of these young girls have and has been killed. And it's not girls that are the target in Jamaica; little boys are targeted also.

Young boys and girls have been molested by family members. Some a di dutty stinking mumma dem wey out dey, noa sey daddy a molest har pickney (daughta) dem an tun a blind eye because of wha. Kacky.

Har pickney di man a abuse. Shi wutless. Di wuse dan slime and crowbait noa sey di man a violate har pickney, an shi a kip har wuse dan armshouse mouth quiet.

THUS THEY VALUE THEIR MEN AND OR MAN KACKY OVA DEM PICKNEY DEM. Yes there is certain things I know about abuse and IT'S TIME WE AS A PEOPLE AND SOCIETY; NATION STOP LETTING THESE MEN TAKE AWAY THE SELF RESPECT AND LIFE OF OUR CHILDREN INCLUDING US AS WOMEN.

There is a code that many black people say they have to up hold like no snitching. There's a code for not snitching. Well bleep that code. **_THIS IS WHY WE ARE ABUSED AND_**

MISUSED. IT'S NOT MONEY OVER LIFE. IT'S LIFE OVER MONEY.

WE HAVE TO STOP MUZZLING THE TRUTH. WE HAVE TO TELL THE TRUTH. WHEN WE KEEP THINGS BOTTLED UP INSIDE IT AFFECTS US MENTALLY AND PHYSICALLY AND WE CANNOT CONTINUE TO LET THESE DEMONS OF THE WORST KIND MUZZLE US AND TRAP US IN HELL.

We have a voice and it's time to use it come on now. I am in pain an di crablouse guh free.

What about my emotional well being?

What about my dignity and self respect.

Everybady come use wi. At the end of the day what the hell do we have?

We as people devalue ourselves and our children. Open your damned mouth. A NATION UNITED CAN NEVER FALL WHEN IT COMES TO TRUTH AND JUSTICE.

Government rape wi, our own rape wi. Wha wi ha lef?

IF YOUR VOICE IS MUZZLED, HOW CAN YOU SPEAK?

IF YOU DON'T STAND UP FOR YOU, WHO WILL STAND UP FOR YOU? IT'S TIME TO RESPECT OURSELVES AND LIVE.

WHEN I KEEP MY MOUTH SHUT, I'M GIVING YOU THE VICTORY OVER ME. WHY THE HELL SHOULD I DO THIS; GIVE YOU MY VICTORY?

You're not Gad and not even Gad want victory over me. But you want my pride; life. Bleep you. Mi a guh tell because death keeps the secret for no one. So why the hell should I keep your secret; the wrongs you've done unto me?

Vegas, we all know the Jamaican Government cares not for the people. They the government devalue the people and none can see this. Lawbreakers break the law and protect the criminals. We all know this, thus many army officials and police officers that has and have done the dirty biddings (wrongs) of them (Government of Jamaica) are safely tucked away in Canada, America, England and some parts of South America and or Latin America to name a few.

It is only when we as human beings start valuing our lives that we will see the difference in it. ***IF YOU GIVE NEGATIVE, ALL YOU WILL GET IS A NEGATIVE OUTCOME.***

This is what many Jamaicans on a whole has and have been given by some of the people and the government out there. Bob Marley did tell us this. Listen to TIME WILL TELL because Jamaicans are truly living in hell. Truly listen to

SAVE THE WORLD by Peetah Morgan because tomorrow does come and Jamaica is doomed because JAMAICA FAILED GOD LITERALLY.

THE SIGN IN THE BLUE AND WHITE SKY SAID, JamaicaF. THUS JAMAICA AND OR JAMAICANS FAILED GOD; ALL.

Like I've said, in your book of death; man's so called holy bible it said, Israel whored and Judah followed suit. So as Israel lost her place with Lovey; Judah (Jamaica) did also. Lovey gave us His flag of life, his name and his breath of life and we lost all three. We lost it without knowing we had it, the truth of him Lovey all around.

No one on the face of this planet; not even the original Jews of Ethiopia had all three, but JAMAICA HAD IT. And yes YOU AMERICA, THE UNITED STATES OF AMERICA HAD THIS BECAUSE YOU HAD THE UPWARD EYE IN TRIANGLE. YOU HAD SPIRITUAL LIFE AND LOST IT. THUS YOU TOO LOST LIFE AND DIDN'T EVEN KNOW IT.

So Mr. Vegas talk the whole and or entire truth and not just a gill bit a eee. Thus Jamaica can be called the pedophile capital of the world. Man just rape off di pickney dem an sometimes kill dem and nothing comes of it; is truly done about it.

Children are not safe in Jamaica. THUS WI NOA BOUT BLACK HEART DEM. Thus di black heart business will neva stop inna di land.

An Vegas, let's not forget the child trafficking wey guane also. Children are being bought and sold and some send to America. A big business in the island. <u>But yet with all the nastiness that guh oone unda di quiet; tourist spend their hard earned money in a dirty and filthy place that has no morals and respect for human dignity and life.</u>

Thus truly good luck to them when DI ROLL IS CALLED BECAUSE MANY ARE GOING TO HEAR DENIED. "YOU'VE DIRTIED SELF BY VACATIONING IN AN UNCLEAN LAND."

Many will ask, why, what land? And they will be told the truth of Jamaica, America and all the lands that were forbidden to them that they went into. Dirty lands that lacked morals, human dignity; good and true life.

Yes I too am fighting with Lovey for there an a nuh one or two time Lovey warn me bout dey. He did tell me out of his own mouth, Jamaica is unclean; dirty and he did show me the sign in the sky that said, JamaicaF; thus Jamaica and Jamaicans did fail him.

Vegas mi done with you now.

Fi unnu man wey sey unnu gay and bleach unnu skin; unnu don't look good. Matterhorn

What the bleep are you things anyway? Thus I put unnu aunda di Transgender It Things category. Unnu nuh gay, unnu gi the gay nation a bad reputation. Thus none of you can categorize unnuself and or put unnuself in the gay world and kingdom. You're not bleeping wanted because unnu sick mi stomach. And yes you of the gay community can tell me to step off because I do not speak for the gay community.

ALSO, STOP DRESSING LIKE FEMALES BECAUSE YOU'RE NOT FEMALES. IT IS A SIN FOR A MAN TO DRESS LIKE A WOMAN. THIS IS A KNOWN FACT, THUS SAITH THE LORD THY GOD MEANING IT IS SO.

You are all male so stop the crap you're doing. NOT ONE OF YOU REPRESENT THE FEMALE GENDER AND RACE AND WE AS FEMALES; WELL SPEAKING FOR MYSELF, I TRULY DO NOT WANT ANY OF YOU REPRESENTING US. YOU CANNOT REPRESENT US AND TRULY DO NOT REPRESENT US. SO STAY THE BLEEP OUT OF OUR GOOD UP, GOOD UP COMMUNITY. TAKE YOUR DRAG QUEEN, SINFUL AND CONDEMNED ASS OUT OF OUR FOLD.

You cannot represent your male counterpart and or self so it is us the good up, good up oman dem yu want come frolic roune. No, I will not have you in our fold. Get the hell out and stay out. You are a damn male act like one.

A true gay male do not act like you. Thus unnu gi gays a bad rep with unnu frounezy self. Unnu wuss dan prostitute because unnu walk street a night anna sell unnu self. Whoring jezebels take off the women's clothing and represent your own male kind. Women do not act like you, nor are WE AS UGLY AND WASHED UP LIKE YOU.

Women did not ask any of you to represent us so truly stay out of our realm with your fake ass self.

No people, I am so fed up of seeing these waste matters on the internet degrading the black race and self.

Some a dem don't have a proper penis but yet dem a pose up demself like dem a sumady.

I know people are entitled to their own opinion but, IS THIS WHAT THE GAY COMMUNITY HAS AND HAVE COME DOWN TO?

Why do we as black people have to make damn fools of ourselves?

When did gayness become immoral?

When did cleanliness leave the gay community and whoredom took fold?

Did we truly forget about XX, XY, 2YX, 3Y and 3XY?

Thus truth have and has been eroded and left for dead.

So for all of you more than rev out it things that call unnu self gay inna Jamaica, truly go chuck and take a good look at yourself on the internet. You are all a disgrace to the black race. ***In fact I truly don't class any of you as black.*** And this goes for some a unnu dragged out funny man (black man) inna di United States. If you are gay, be gay, but stop degrading yourself. Stop degrading the female gender because we are not degrading you.

You are not females. You are a male so represent the male gender appropriately. No wonder many people don't like gays.

Kiss mi yass now man. Move. Unna a man act like such thus you have a penis not a vagina. And not even a woman with a vagina act like unnu.

Set a crosses that plague humanity with your nastiness. Be yourself not someone that you are not. And anyone gay come to me and say I am bashing gays take a stick and truly bash on it by rotating it up in you.

Man sey dem gay anna cuss man. Whore sidung. Coo pan unnu to. Beach out and lacking morals.

None of you look good. Di duppy an di demons of hell look better dan unnu to yass.

Not even di demons of hell want unnu. Anna a suh man fool fool fi lay dung with sinting lacka unnu.

I guess man will lay with anything to yass. Thus my venting is done for now.

No for real people, truly take a look at the internet and see what I am talking about. A man must be a man.

Man a cuss man ova dem owna things?

Wow we oman cuss but demya sinting ya truly take the cake to yass. Thus these things need to truly clean up self and get a good and true life.

Stop degrading yourself now man come on now. So what if you are gay. Go about your own business and stop broadcasting your nasty and dirty prostitution lifestyle to the world. Have some moral values for your lifestyle and self.

Michelle Jean

Oh man I am so tired of writing. So I am going to end this book with Bob Marley's TIME WILL TELL and not SAVE THE WORLD by Peetah Morgan or FULLFILMENT TIME by Tony Tuff and Smokie Benz.

OTHER BOOKS BY MICHELLE JEAN

Blackman Redemption – The Fall of Michelle Jean
Blackman Redemption – After the Fall Apology
Blackman Redemption – World Cry – Christine Lewis
Blackman Redemption
Blackman Redemption – The Rise and Fall of Jamaica
Blackman Redemption – The War of Israel
Blackman Redemption – The Way I Speak to God
Blackman Redemption – A Little Talk With Man
Blackman Redemption – The Den of Thieves
Blackman Redemption – The Death of Jamaica
Blackman Redemption – Happy Mother's Day
Blackman Redemption – The Death of Faith
Blackman Redemption – The War of Religion
Blackman Redemption – The Death of Russia
Blackman Redemption – The Truth
Blackman Redemption – Spiritual War
Blackman Redemption – The Youths
Blackman Redemption – Black Man Where Is Your God?

The New Book of Life
The New Book of Life – A Cry For The Children
The New Book of Life – Judgement
The New Book of Life – Love Bound
The New Book of Life – Me
The New Book of Life – Life

Just One of Those Days
Book Two – Just One of Those Days
Just One of Those Days – Book Three The Way I Feel
Just One of Those Days – Book Four

The Days I Am Weak
Crazy Thoughts – My Book of Sin
Broken
Ode to Mr. Dean Fraser

A Little Little Talk
A Little Little Talk – Book Two

Prayers
My Collective
A Little Talk/A Time For Fun and Play
Simple Poems
Behind The Scars
Songs of Praise And Love

Love Bound
Love Bound – Book Two

Dedication Unto My Kids
More Talk
Saving America From A Woman's Perspective
My Collective the Other Side of Me
My Collective the Dark Side of Me
A Blessed Day
Lose To Win
My Doubtful Days – Book One

My Little Talk With God
My Little Talk With God – Book Two

A Different Mood and World – Thinking

My Nagging Day
My Nagging Day – Book Two

Friday September 13, 2013
My True Love
It Would Be You
My Day

A Little Advice – Talk
1313, 2032, 2132 – The End of Man
Tata

MICHELLE'S BOOK BLOG – BOOKS 1 – 20

My Problem Day
A Better Way
Stay – Adultery and the Weight of Sin – Cleanliness
Message

Let's Talk
Lonely Days – Foundation
A Little Talk With Jamaica – As Long As I Live
Instructions For Death
My Lonely Thoughts
My Lonely Thoughts – Book Two
My Morning Talks – Prayers With God
What A Mess
My Little Book
A Little Word With You
My First Trip of 2015
Black Mother – Mama Africa
Islamic Thought
My California Trip January 2015
My True Devotion by Michelle – Michelle Jean
My Many Questions To God
My Talk
My Talk Book Two

My Talk Book Three – The Rise of Michelle Jean
My Talk Book Four
My Talk Book Five
My Talk Book Six
My Talk Book Seven
My Talk Book Eight – My Depression
My Talk Book Nine – Death
My Talk Book Ten – Wow
My Day – Book Two
My Talk Book Eleven – What About December?
Haven Hill
What About December – Book Two
My Talk Book Twelve – Summary and or Confusion